Catherine Owen

**A key to Cooking : that will unlock many kitchen Mysteries**

wrought out and made ready for Public use

Catherine Owen

**A key to Cooking : that will unlock many kitchen Mysteries**
*wrought out and made ready for Public use*

ISBN/EAN: 9783744789806

Printed in Europe, USA, Canada, Australia, Japan

Cover: Foto ©Lupo / pixelio.de

More available books at **www.hansebooks.com**

THAT WILL UNLOCK MANY KITCHEN MYSTERIES.


WROUGHT OUT AND MADE READY
FOR PUBLIC USE.


———————


By CATHERINE OWEN.


———————

CLARK W. BRYAN & COMPANY, PUBLISHERS,
HOLYOKE, MASS.
NEW YORK OFFICE, 239 BROADWAY.

# PREFACE.

Some chapters of this little book appeared in *Scribner's Magazine* (20th volume). The whole is the result of much reading, from Grimod de la Reyniere of the last century, to the much more instructive and scientific authorities of the present generation. It is not, however, simply a student's digest or "boiling down" of all the volumes written on the subject. The reading was accompanied by patient practice and experiment, (and alas, many failures,) with nothing to turn to but books for help, and books which were written for those who were already adepts. Helps, in case of failure or suggestions of its possibility, there were none. At that time cooking schools, with their perfect mastery of the subject and their demonstration of processes, were only beginning to be thought of.

I believe that if I could have found the rules of the best authorities for the different processes of cooking shortly stated, instead of having to seek and compare, learning to cook scientifically—that is to obtain sure results from a given process—might have been a business of a few months instead of years.

It was these failures and this belief which have induced me to republish and enlarge this series of papers, which contain the summing up of all there is to be learned of the theory and practice of good plain cooking, gathered from very many volumes published during the last hundred years.

I do not think anything I shall ever be able to write, will be more valuable to the inexperienced cook, than this little contribution to the literature of what a French poet calls the "dainty art."

CATHERINE OWEN.

# INDEX.

# TABLE OF WEIGHTS AND MEASURES.

The subjoined table of weights and measures is given for use only where approximate quantities are sufficiently exact. For all fine cooking accurate proportions are necessary, and many dishes should not be attempted without a good scale which will weigh half and quarter ounces. *Exactness in details is the soul of good cooking*, and it is the inveterate habit of measuring by cups, that destroys much well meant effort. Use the scales often and weighing will soon become as easy as measuring.

One pint of granulated sugar is . . one pound.
One quart of flour is . . . . one pound.
Eight tablespoonfuls of liquid are . . . one gill.
Four gills are . . . . . . . . . . one pint.
One level tablespoonful of butter is . . one ounce.
One full tablespoon of flour is . . . . one ounce.
Four small teaspoonfuls are . one large tablespoonful.
Two teaspoonfuls are . . . . one dessertspoonful.
One teacup averages rather over . . . one gill.
One kitchen cup is . . . . . half a pint.

# A KEY TO COOKING.

## CHAPTER I.

### *General Principles of Cookery.*

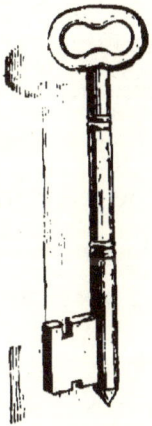

T is not intended in this little book to give general recipes. Such as may be given are meant to illustrate general principles of cookery, or else to meet such difficulties as cookery books often raise ; the intention is to aid rather than to supersede more formal directions. A good cookery book is a useful ally to the most experienced cook; to the tyro it is often but a blind guide; without a knowledge of the first principles of cooking this is inevitable. Who does not remember poor Bella in "Our Mutual Friend,"—her elbows on the table, her temples in her hands, consulting with all the eager zeal of a newly-made matron, the "Complete British Housewife," and finding her poor little brains quite unable to cope with the sibylline mysteries therein propounded, exclaiming—

" Oh, you ridiculous old thing, what *do* you mean by that ?"

The few rules, a knowledge of which make successful cooking from a book easy, can fortunately be briefly explained and easily remembered. The plain boiling, roasting, frying, and stewing are what make really good cooking; and it is safe to say that the woman who knows how to do these well, need never fear for her dinner table.

The trouble, in these days, is not with the cooking books—there are several that are all that could be desired in the way of minute direction. Those who write them no longer tell you to "take some of this," "a handful of that." The women of the present day who have written on cooking, have done so from exact knowledge, and given directions with such precision that if the *rules for cooking* are known there is little chance of mistake.

But—and in this "but" lies the gist of the matter— how few know these rules, how very few think it necessary to know them—a good recipe seems all that is needed. The recipe is really of little avail, unless you know how to use it. The recipe for a boiled pudding may be excellent, but unless you know how to boil puddings in general, the pudding may be spoilt. True, with good recipes and that popular kitchen fetich "luck," your kitchen operations *may* turn out well—or, they may not. With a knowledge of the principles of cookery, and their scrupulous observance, they *must* turn out well. It would be a very difficult matter for any one to work out an example in fractions, without knowing the first four rules of arithmetic; yet a woman serenely goes to work with a cooking book, without any knowledge of the few rules (not half so hard to learn as those rules of arithmetic) of cooking—which if she did know, would make success certain—is naturally worried with uncertainty from the beginning, and in the end, if the end be failure, cannot understand the cause of it; consequently she learns nothing from her first attempts. While to the woman *who knows*, a failure will be a lesson; she can see the cause and avoid it afterwards.

What she has to know and remember are rules for the following processes of cooking:

*Boiling*—and the difference between boiling of meat, of vegetables, of puddings.

*Roasting and Baking.*
*Broiling.*
*Stewing.*
*Frying.*

Nevertheless the utility of knowing these rules thoroughly will depend much on whether she will also stop to think of them, as applied to her recipes. Will she remember that if she can make good clear beef soup she can make a dozen varieties of soup—by simply modifying flavorings, or changing the vermicelli she may use at one time, for rice, or noodles, or shredded vegetables, at another?  Will she remember that if she knows the two "Mother Sauces," as they are aptly called by the French—white sauce and brown (Spanish)—that she can make a dozen of the costly and high sounding sauces that belong to high class cooking—by simply following a recipe?  While, if the white sauce in its simple form is lumpy or pasty, she can make none properly, even though she may use all the materials that go to make White Sauce into *Allemande*, or *Poulette*, or *Hollandaise*.

It is the same with roasting meat.  The principle of quick browning once understood, and that the presence of steam in the oven prevents browning, (if the oven is too hot it also prevents burning, in which case its presence is useful), and there will be an end of pallid joints on the table.

And so with frying, boiling, etc—to do one thing of a kind *perfectly*, and *know why* it is perfect, is to hold the key to all things of that kind.  In short, in cooking, as in many other arts, the first steps well understood, the seemingly more difficult achievements become surprisingly clear and easy.

# CHAPTER II.

*Boiling—The Right Way, and the Wrong Way.*

THE first branch to take up is boiling, because it is the branch of which people seem to know least. How rare it is to find this simple operation well done! How often we hear it said of boiled beef or ham, for instance, " Fine flavor, but so tough," and how few people know that the toughness proceeds, in nine cases out of ten, from quick boiling! In the case of ham, that most abused of all joints, and perhaps the easiest of all to cook, your cookery book probably tells you to boil it slowly four, five, or six hours, according to size; and people usually interpret this direction into putting the ham into the pot, and letting it boil at what is actually a slow gallop for the given time; while

very often, if entrusted to a cook, it boils only at intervals.
So that it remains on the fire a given number of hours,
Chloe or Bridget thinks the boiling is done.  Ham should
not boil, it should merely simmer.  A fair sized ham put
on at ten in the morning, if properly cooked, should be
done and tender by four or five in the afternoon.  The
water should be brought to the boiling point, which
means *just beginning* to *boil*, indicated by an occasional
bubble, the pot then be set back on the stove, and the
water be allowed to simmer.  The ham should be turned
in the water once or twice during the time it is on the
fire.  When sufficiently done it should cool in the
water, unless required for eating hot, the rind should be
stripped from it, and the ham well dusted with sifted
bread crumbs, made by baking slices of bread in a slow
oven until they are of a fine golden brown all through,
and dry enough to powder under the rolling pin.  Never
stick your ham with cloves ; it suggests flies, and spoils
the flavor for many tastes.  A pretty finish is given by
dusting it well with sugar instead of bread, and then
passing a hot knife over it until it has melted and
coated the ham with a caramel glaze.  A much finer
way is to glaze it with strong meat jelly, or any savory
jelly you may have, boiled down rapidly until it is like
glue, taking great care during this boiling-down process

to prevent burning. This jelly should be brushed over the ham when cool; it makes a handsome dish of a plain one.

The same rule of boiling holds good with beef. Corned beef is generally a hard, salt, dry fare: but, properly cooked, it should be more tender than roast meat, and almost as juicy. In order that any boiled meat shall be tender, it is necessary to remember that the boiling must be slow. Different people have given such different interpretations to the expression, "slow boiling," that it is well to be explicit. Most people think that if the whole surface of the water is in a state of slow ebullition, this is slow boiling. For boiling meat, a great French authority gives this rule, which I have found excellent: The ebullition should only appear in one part of the surface of the water, and there be only just visible. This is, however, distinct from stewing, or simmering, which is yet slower, there being in that process no ebullition, but merely a sizzling on one side of the stew-pan.

Authorities differ as to whether meat should be put into hot or cold water; many books omit all direction on this subject. My own rule is to plunge fresh or slightly salt meat into boiling water allowing it to boil fast five minutes, then to simmer, in order to retain the juices. For this reason highly salted or soup meat I put into *cold* water, that the salt in the one case, and the gravy in the other, may be drawn out.

What has been said about the boiling of meats does not apply to vegetables. For them, with few exceptions, quick boiling is necessary. It may be taken as a rule that all green vegetables. such as cabbage, Brussels sprouts, string beans, etc., should be boiled quickly in abundance of water.

*Cabbage*, as usually served, is a coarse, rank vegetable, while properly cooked, fresh cabbage is as delicate and delicious as cauliflower. Cut it into four or six pieces, put these into a large saucepan with plenty of boiling water, and let them be brought quickly to the boiling point, and kept rapidly boiling with the cover off, for 25 minutes, pushing the leaves down with a spoon as they rise above the water. Let it boil thus until quite tender, but no longer, as the vegetable then loses color and flavor, and becomes rank, yellow, and wilted.

This method of allowing abundance of water and space, together with quick boiling, does not apply to peas. spinach, and asparagus.

*Peas* require only moderately quick boiling in sufficient water to cover them, to which has been added a spoonful of sugar, not enough to sweeten, but only to replace the sweetness the water has taken away. English people always add a small bunch of fresh mint.

*Asparagus* requires special care, and after it has been scraped and trimmed (cutting an inch or two, if it is long, from the root end) it should be tied in bundles and put to stand in a deep saucepan, with water just reaching to the tops. It should then be boiled with moderate quickness until done. *i. e.*, for about twenty minutes. You will then find that you can take it up without losing one of the frail heads, and the flavor is much fuller than when these have been soaked by lying down in the water. Always have a slice of toast at the bottom of your vegetable dish for asparagus or cauliflower; it drains those delicate vegetables better than you can otherwise do without injuring them.

*Spinach* is another vegetable that is rarely well cooked; it is of such a watery nature that it should be put into the pot in which it is to be boiled without water; it will soon make enough liquid with its own juice; when tender, take it out, chop and season it: meanwhile allow the juice that remains in the saucepan to boil down; then return the spinach to it, and stew until the excess of liquid is evaporated. Put less salt to this vegetable than to others. It is hardly necessary to say, perhaps, that vegetables must always be boiled in salted water.

To sum up, the rules for boiling then are these:

*Highly Salted or Smoked Meats to be put into cold water and* allowed to come to the boiling point very slowly.

*Fresh or Lightly Salted Meat and Poultry to go into boiling water.* Allowed to boil fast for a minute or two, then kept just at the boiling point till done.

*Fish must not be allowed to boil fast,* even at first, or it may break, the violent motion caused by rapid ebullition being sufficient to cause this in delicate fish.

*Vegetables require putting into plenty of salted, fast boiling water, to be rapidly brought back to the fast boiling condition, and kept at it till done.*

On no account must any vegetable be allowed only to simmer, or, as is often done, *to soak* for an hour or so on the range in water below boiling point. They will be strong, rank and sodden under such treatment, in fact the vegetable as it is served nine times out of ten. Nor must they be overdone, cabbage in winter takes half an hour at most, and twenty minutes in summer, in spite of the fact that it is usually spoiled by hours of boiling.

The exceptions to this rapid boiling of vegetables are:

CAULIFLOWER AND ASPARAGUS, because they are liable to suffer from the rapid motion of the water and break; but they must nevertheless boil steadily, but not so fast as to send them whirling round in the water.

PEAS, because the same rapid motion may burst the skins.

POTATOES, because quick boiling will cause the outer layers of a fine mealy potato to break and dissolve in the water while the inside is still hard. For this reason potatoes are best poured dry the moment they are tender, and left to steam two or three minutes in the saucepan with the cover on. Then give the saucepan one or two gentle rolling shakes, and remove the cover; the shaking breaks the outer surface of the potato and the escaping steam covers it with a floury coat.

FOR CABBAGE AND STRING OR GREEN BEANS, if the water is not very soft, use a salt spoonful of baking soda to each gallon. (*Be careful never to overdo the quantity.*)

PUDDINGS. *Any kind of pudding must be plunged into rapidly boiling water, brought back to the same stage as quickly as possible, and kept fast boiling every minute of the time it is in the water.*

I have used the terms "boiling point" and "fast boiling" in the general, not the scientific, sense. The "boiling point" is actually some degrees below boiling, the rapid boiling is *only* boiling; it is impossible without special superheating appliances to make water hotter than boiling point, that is 212° Fah. Therefore, it is the fact that the water is actually "boiling" water, which hardens the albumen in meat, rendering it tough, while water at "boiling point," *i. e.*, scientifically some degrees *below* it, is the right degree for boiling meat, because the albumen does not harden, and the meat, therefore, is tender and juicy.

Some interesting experiments which *prove* what to many may seem mere theory, are given in Mr. Matthieu Williams's delightfully written and valuable *Chemistry of Cooking*, to which I refer every earnest woman who wishes to know the why and wherefore of kitchen operations. Once having read and digested that book, a cooking book would cease to be the doubtful aid it now is.

# CHAPTER III.

*Directions for Making Soups.*

WITTY Frenchman says : "To make good soup, the pot should scarcely smile." This is as true of stewing meat, as of making soup. To do either well, the whole process must be exceedingly slow, from beginning to end ; the saucepan should only "*smile*."

To make good soup, the meat should be put on in cold water, and slowly brought to the boil, that the juices may be drawn out. Before it comes to the boiling point, the scum will rise freely : take it off before ebullition has broken and scattered it; then when it does boil, throw in half a cup of water, and skim again —add this water just as it comes to the boil two or three times; it brings all remaining scum rapidly to the suface, and when this rises no longer, set aside to simmer. It must never go below simmering point after this until made. This is the whole secret of clear soup. I will here give Jules Gouffé's receipt for *Pot-au-feu* ; if carefully followed, a clear, pale bouillon will be the result, and this bouillon is the foundation of most soups. Boiled down to one-half its bulk it becomes *consommé.*

*Pot-au-feu* requires four pounds of beef without bones, six quarts of water, six ounces of carrot, six ounces of turnip, same quantity of onions, three ounces of celery and two cloves. After once or twice making this soup, the cook will be able to judge by the size of the vegetables the required quantity, but weighing is advisable at first, as much depends on perfect proportion. The meat must slowly simmer for three hours, then add the vegetables, not before; simmer till done. With bone and beef together, four quarts of water to four pounds of meat.

Quick boiling and careless skimming are the causes of cloudy bouillon; supposing, as a matter of course, that all the vegetables have been perfectly cleansed.

For soup the rules are few and simple. *Cold water must be put on the meat in the proportion of one quart to one pound of ordinary soup meat and bone.* If solid meat is used, a quart and a pint may be allowed. This, when strained, may be boiled down to any required strength, but will be found strong enough as a prelude to dinner when clear, fragrant bouillon, rather than concentrated nourishment is required.

The reason for putting meat in cold water for soup is

because the object is *to draw out* the juices; *for this reason it should take at least two hours before it reaches the boiling point.*

*The vegetables should be very carefully proportioned.*

The same rules apply to making soup from bones.

*Rule for thickening White Soups and Fricassees : For thickening white soups the proportion is one tablespoonful (not heaped, nor yet quite level.) of flour and one tablespoonful of butter to each quart of liquid. If eggs are added it must be after the soup is entirely made and ready for table. They should be beaten and mixed with a cup of the soup that has slightly cooled,* then stirred into the whole of it which must on no account be allowed *to boil* after they are added, but must come to *the boiling point* (or they will be raw,) and immediately poured out. The cause of "breaking" or curdling is the fact that they have boiled. This same rule applies to fricassee in which eggs are used, or anything cooked à la Poulette.

*For thickening brown soups the proportion is also one tablespoonful of flour to the quart.*

The "boiling point," which I have said elsewhere is only the beginning of boiling, is indicated by an *occasional* bubble from the center of the pot, which breaks and spreads in hardly perceptible circles on the water— the French "smile."

It often happens that soup intended to be brown is not sufficiently so even when made very strong, to be inviting without coloring. Caramel is generally used for this purpose ; but onions cut in slices and left in a moderate oven until they are black chips (not charred, however,) may be kept bottled for this purpose; a small quantity added to a stew or soup improves the flavor ; or, they may be fried each time and added with the other vegetables.

For white stock use veal or fowls instead of beef.

# CHAPTER IV.

*Stewing—and How to Make Stews.*

THERE are brown, highly flavored stews, which are called ragouts, in which the meat is browned before stewing, and white ones, mildly flavored, which should have cream or be thickened with eggs, and although technically known by a variety of names, according to variations in the preparation, are commonly classed under the term "fricassees."

*For Ragouts,* the meat should be wiped dry and quickly browned with a little butter or its own fat cut small and first fried out. The vegetables also should be dry and browned with the meat. In order to thus brown them, the stewpan must be first made hot. If the meat be tough or old poultry is used, it will be made tender by first being brushed over with vinegar, and allowed to remain with the vinegar on it for several hours; or, after it is browned, a tablespoonful of vinegar may be put to it, and the pot covered closely and set where it will steam, not boil, for an hour before the water is added. After it is cooked there will be no more flavor of vinegar than the pleasant dash of acid characteristic of French cookery. The acid possesses the property of dissolving the tough fiber.

No more water should ever be put to the meat than is required to serve for gravy. Half a pint to each pound of meat is usually enough.

In stewing, as the meat is to be eaten. the object is not to draw out the juices, hence the quick carbonizing or browning of the outer surface which helps to retain them, as well as enhancing the flavor. Hot water should be put on meat for a stew, and if the process is properly slow, very little will be lost by evaporation therefore very little extra need be allowed. Putting a quantity of water and allowing it to boil away. is the primitive manner of stewing, which produces such poor results.

Ragged meat from long stewing is not necessarily tender; the fibres it is true are so disintegrated. that it can be separated with a fork, but each separate fibre may be peculiarly tough, this is when the stewing, has been really, fast boiling, the length of time only having dissolved the gelatinous tissues.

The rules for making stews then are these:

*The meat must have only enough water to serve as gravy, not to form a broth.*

That if any coarse or tough meat is used. it will be made tender and more savory by first allowing it to brown quickly and then steaming with a little acid (vinegar or lemon juice) before adding water, which must be boiling.

When tender meat is used, as young birds, this preliminary steaming is not necessary.

*The whole process must be a gentle simmer.*

*To simmer means to cook more slowly than boiling.* In *slow boiling* the heat comes from the *center* of the pot which indicates a greater degree of heat than *simmering, which is only a gentle sizzling round the edge of the saucepan*—watch for a few minutes to find out the part of your range on which this point can be best kept up.

The flavor of a stew depends much on the thickening. Use brown thickening or white thickening (see recipes) instead of raw flour and butter to ragouts or fricassees. (Try both methods at once. dividing your meat; it will be very little extra trouble, and the experience gained will teach more than all my writing, and will repay you.)

It was not my intention to give any recipes in this little book because it is only intended as an aid to a cooking book, but as several otherwise good cooking books do not contain recipes for the brown and white thickenings, to which I have referred, I have appended them.

*Brown Thickening or Roux:* Put a half pound of butter in a small frying-pan, or saucepan, enameled or iron, not tin. Let it melt, skim it, then stir into it half a pound of dried and sifted flour. Let this cook until it is a bright pale golden brown, stirring constantly so that it may not get at all burnt. When done, put it away in a pot for use. A spoonful of this stirred into a stew, or gravy, or soup to thicken it, gives a rich smoothness, very different from that of the usual flour and water thickening, hastily stirred in at the last moment: and any one who knows what a hindrance those little things done at the last moment are, will realize, the convenience of brown thickening, although its use by professional cooks does not come from convenience, but from its superior flavor.

*White Thickening* is half a pound of butter melted and skimmed, and half a pound of sifted flour dredged into it, and allowed to bubble together, stirring it till it is quite cooked and no raw flour smell remains, but it must not be allowed to color. This also is to be put away in a pot, and used for thickening white stews, fricassees, or dressing vegetables as will be hereafter directed.

# CHAPTER V.

*Roasting—How to Do It Well.*

IT is very common to find things that are proverbially easy to do, less well done than those of acknowledged difficulty, simply because it is taken as a foregone conclusion that no art at all is required. Yet, as Mrs. Gamp says, "There's art in sticking in a pin," and in roasting meat, although it will be a new idea to many, there is at least the art of simplicity, if I may so speak ; and Brillat-Savarin says : "One may become a cook, but must be born a roaster," which implies that genius is required to roast well; however, common-sense and a persevering attention to rules are not bad substitutes. It is the common practice to put a quantity of water in the pan with meat to roast, and to make a bad thing worse, the joint is thickly dredged with flour. On asking a cook, who had thrown a handful of flour over a sirloin of beef and then poured a quart of water into the pan with it, what was the object of such immersion, she answered with an air of good-natured contempt for our ignorance:

" For the gravy, of course, ma'm! Where would I get my gravy if I didn't do that?"

Of course meat so treated comes to table sodden, juiceless, tasteless, and unsightly, and accompanied by a quart—more or less—of gray, thickish broth, instead of the rich brown gravy natural to well-cooked meat.

In addition to this flour-and-water treatment, the abused joint is often put into a lukewarm oven an hour or two before it begins to cook, where it slowly steams and oozes, until the hour for dinner, when, whether it is cooked little or much, it is served.

Roasting, then, as I have hinted, must be very simple. Little or no preparation is necessary. The only requisites are a bright fire and a hot oven; then place the joint in the pan, on an iron tripod if possible, as this keeps it out of the fat; little flour not over a teaspoonful is necessary if the meat has not been washed, and if you buy from a good butcher this will be needed only in summer if it has been kept an hour or two too long; then wash it off with vinegar, dry it carefully, and very lightly dust it with flour to absorb any moisture that may remain on the surface. While the meat is in the oven, baste it several times, and when about half done, turn it—always keeping the thickest part of the meat in the hottest part of the oven.

In cooking a sirloin of beef great care must be taken that the fat of the "undercut," as our English cousins call it, be quite cooked. It is not unusual to see a splendid roast come to the table with the fat of the tenderloin not even warm through, and the tender meat of that favorite part absolutely purple, while the upper and less choice part is sufficiently cooked.

While the meat is in the oven the fire should be kept hot and bright; it should have been so made up as to last sufficiently long, but if the joint is very large it may require replenishing, this may be done without checking the heat of the oven, by adding a little fuel from time to time, instead of waiting until it requires a great deal.

If the oven has been in good condition, the meat will be beautifully brown and the bottom of the pan covered with a thick glaze. Gently pour off the fat, holding the pan steadily as you do it, that the gravy may not go with it; then put the pan on the stove and pour into it half a cup of boiling water (more if the joint is very large and less if very small) and a little salt. If you have soup of any kind, use it in preference to water: stir it with a spoon until the adhering glaze or gravy is entirely removed from the pan, it will dissolve as it mingles with the liquid, and make a rich brown gravy.

Before the joint is served, sift over it evenly—not in patches—fine salt. This must never be done before it is cooked, as it draws out the juice of the meat.

It must be repeated, that nothing so injures meat as to put it into a cool oven, allowing both to get hot together.

Some meats require longer to cook than others. Pork and veal much longer than mutton and beef. The former meats require to be very well done—the latter. most people like under-done; but even when this is the case, it should be remembered, that the texture should be changed all through; the gravy is then released and runs red with the knife, while the grain of the meat is seen through it, of a bright red instead of the livid purple hue so frequently called rare, but which is simply raw.

Poultry may be either cooked with a little butter to baste it, or it may be larded or "barded."

All white-fleshed birds are improved by larding, as are veal and sweetbreads. Yet small ones, quails, for instance, may have a barde—*i. e.*, a slice of bacon fat—tied round them. This may also be done with fowls, or veal, where bacon is liked and larding inconvenient.

Game requires nothing but good butter to baste it. Any sort of stuffing is ruinous to the flavor, except in the case of pigeons, where a little chopped parsley may be mixed with butter, and placed inside.

Wild duck, if fishy, and the flavor is disliked, should be scalded for a few minutes in salt and water before roasting. If the flavor is very strong the duck may be skinned, as the oil in the skin is the objectionable part. After skinning, spread with butter, and thickly dredge with flour before putting in a very quick oven.

The rules for roasting are :

*A hot oven when first the meat goes in*, the smaller the joint the hotter it should be, if the joint is very small it should be hot enough to brown the meat all over in a very short time, so as to seal up the juices and prevent it being dry.

*To brown thoroughly all over, put no water in the pan*, but if the oven is likely to burn at the bottom and so destroy the gravy and dripping, slip an extra sheet of tin under the pan or set your dripping pan in another one. If your oven " catches " and is apt to burn it is a good plan to put a vessel containing water in it as the steam will prevent the burning.

*Frequent basting.* If the meat is too dry to admit of this, put some nice dripping in the pan, taking care not to use *mutton* dripping for the purpose, unless the meat be mutton, which however seldom needs it. *Poultry and game require a very hot oven indeed, and to be well basted.*

# CHAPTER VI.

## *Frying.—Keep the Fat Hot.*

BRILLAT-SAVARIN says, in an account of a conversation with his cook, " You are an excellent *potagiste*, [*i. e.*, soup-maker], but are weak in the matter of frying." This weakness is common to so many cooks, and his directions are so clear and concise, that the quotation may be continued : "The chief element of success in frying is the *surprise*"—a very French and very graphic way of stating the fact. "To produce this, the fat must be sufficiently hot." When the meat is browned, "draw back the pan, that the cooking may not be too quick—that the juices, which have been sealed up, may in the slower process undergo the changes necessary to blend them and give them flavor."

Inexperienced cooks are apt to think that as soon as fat begins to bubble up it is hot enough, and that it will burn if left longer over the fire. Burnt fat would of course, ruin everything, but the danger of burning is less than might be supposed. The fat should not only bubble but begin to smoke. A degree of heat less than this will cause potatoes to wilt, looking brown on one side and pallid on the other. Fish will be freckled with brown, with a gelatinous skin and greasy flesh. To test whether the fat is hot enough, when the "sizzling" has ceased for some time, and the smoke begins to appear, drop a small square of bread into it; if the bread crisps and browns at once, put in your fish or cutlets immediately. If the bread causes only a quiet "sizzling," and does not brown in a few seconds, the fat is not hot enough.

Breaded chops, cutlets, etc., are often thought to be unattainable luxuries in families where inexperienced cooks are the rule. The result is too often, it is true, a greasy, piebald failure. Yet with finely-grated bread crumbs, and with due attention to the *surprise*—that is, to having the fat very hot and an abundance of it— nothing is easier to do well. The bread-crumbs and egg come off, for one of three reasons: The fat is not hot enough, or there is not enough of it in the pan, or else the bread-crumbs are too coarse or uneven. If you have no bread stale enough to crumble finely, dry out some slices in a cool oven or use cracker meal. Let the article to be fried be perfectly dry.

The rules for perfect frying are:

*Abundance of fat in a deep kettle.*
**The fat to be far beyond the "boiling point," or what is**

called so—the *appearance* of boiling (which only comes from the moisture in the fat) being very deceptive and the cause of half the bad frying.

*The fat must smoke from the center.* It will smoke from the sides long before it is hot enough.

Put the fat on the range some time before it is needed: for it takes a very much longer time to heat, than is generally supposed.

Remember *if the fat is hot enough,* the cooking is done in one quarter the time of frying with a little fat; a chop breaded will cook in *two minutes* and be beautifully brown: oysters in *one minute.* Then it is more economical, for the two pounds of lard if strained (after it has slightly cooled) through cheese cloth, will serve many times and reduces very little. It is more healthful for the intense heat closes up all pores—and none of the gravy escapes, nor does any of the fat enter the articles fried. If they are greasy, then be sure they have been put into the fat long before it was hot enough, and left in it some time to brown. This is not what is meant. The article, even, if not to be quickly fried, as doughnuts or fried cakes, should *brown instantly* to keep out the grease—then if they need slower cooking *when they are brown, draw them back a very little way.*

*If you try frying in deep fat and your fish or what not, does not brown all over beautifully in less than two minutes, your fat was not hot enough,* perhaps not nearly so. Take this as a rule, and don't be afraid of the burning point, for the instant you drop in one article it checks that.

Never try frying in fat that has been once used, without it has been strained, or you will find your dainty dish disfigured by dark particles.

# CHAPTER VII.

*Broiling—A Favorite Method of Cooking.*

ITH English and Americans, broiling is a favorite mode of dressing meat and fish. On the continent, where frying is so perfectly done as to be healthful, it is less popular. To broil well is considered a test of a cook's skill, and is undoubtedly a test of her carefulness. A bright, hot fire, yet not too hot, a smooth, clean gridiron, and attention to one or two points, can scarcely fail to give good results. Chops or steaks should be neither salted nor peppered before they are broiled. If very lean, they will be better dipped in a little butter, which has been made hot in a plate. Turn the meat very soon after it has been put on the fire, and continue to turn frequently, until done. (The dampers should be always first turned back, that the odor may go up the chimney.) If there is any danger of burning, throw some salt on the fire and raise the gridiron.

Always have ready a hot dish, and a cover, also

heated. For steaks or fish, have a good piece of butter, with pepper and salt in the dish.

Small birds should be strung on a skewer, not too closely together, first having been rubbed over with butter. They should be served on buttered toast.

Chickens are difficult to broil well, without either burning or leaving the joints raw. To avoid this, first break the bones slightly with a rolling-pin, that they may lie flat, and put the chickens in the oven for a short time. Then rub them over with butter, and broil until crisp and brown. Covering them with a saucepan lid will also concentrate the heat and help to cook them thoroughly through, without burning; turn them frequently, and baste with a brush or feather dipped in warm butter. All broiled dishes should be served very hot.

Fish may be cooked in the same way, rubbing the bars of the gridiron with suet or salt, to prevent them sticking. A clear fire, quite free from smoke or flame, is necessary to broil well, but *when the flame comes from the meat fat* it is quite different from coal flame, and the great mistake is to raise the meat and try to blow out that flame—then a dense smoke comes—and this *blackens* the meat; the flame *browns* it. Therefore, keep the meat, unless very thick, quite close to the fire, *immersed* in the flame, rather than *above* it to catch the smoke, which if your flues are open will go up the chimney. Let the broiler tilt toward the chimney or back of range.

Blackened smoky broiling, as often comes from too much care as too little; the cook is afraid of the flame.

The rules for good broiling are:

A hot fire.

A quick draught.

*A bold disregard of the flame, a careful avoidance of smoke.* (Smoke or flame there will be, unless the meat is very lean.)

*Care not to overcook.*

A well cooked chop or steak is *plump* ; if it sinks under the finger in a flabby way, it is still very rare : if it springs up again, it is medium; if it is firm, it is very well or overdone—at this stage it will not be plump, but rather shrunken and dry.

It is well to lay it *for one instant* on a piece of hot manilla or common kitchen paper, so that any dark drippings may be received by that, then transfer it to a hot dish at once and season.

# CHAPTER VIII.

## *Sauces—White Sauce and Brown Sauce.*

THE characteristics of fine white or brown sauce (and most others) are smoothness, a rich well cooked flavor, and a consistency that is neither so thick as to be pasty, nor so thin as to run off the article covered with it. It should coat it with a heavy cream-like surface, but not be so thick that it will not run unless helped to do so with a spoon. To secure this consistency and smoothness and absence of raw taste, the following are the rules:

*Allow one ounce of flour and one ounce of butter to each half pint of liquid.* (One average tablespoonful is equivalent to an ounce.)

*Stir flour and butter together in a thick saucepan over the fire,* and let it bubble till it no longer smells of raw flour—as long in fact as you can without burning it. Have the half pint of milk or broth boiling hot, and pour it *quickly* to the flour and butter, stirring all the while, just as you would make starch. If the liquid is slowly added it will thicken too fast, and may be lumpy. The sauce will be thick and smooth; let it boil one minute at the back of the stove; if necessary to keep it hot do so in boiling water. This sauce may have more butter stirred in after it has boiled, if wanted very rich, but the quantity of flour must never be increased. For all other kinds of white sauce this is the foundation, and if you think over many French recipes as you read them, you will be surprised to find that it is also the foundation for many other things, as fondu, and several dishes of cheese, croquettes, confectioner's cream, etc.

## Brown Sauce.

The rules are the same as to proportions, but the butter and flour are allowed to cook together till they are *pale* brown, and soup or gravy takes the place of milk. Then it is ready to be made into piquante, mushroom, poivrade, matelote or Robert sauce, according to your recipe, or to be used simply as brown or Spanish sauce. Of course, if you are *thinking* on the subject, you will see that chopped meat or fish moistened with either brown or white sauce becomes the finest kind of hash.

# Chapter IX.

## *Warming Over Meats, etc.*

OILEAU declares, emphatically, that "A warmed-over dinner is never good for anything," in which he is entirely wrong. There are some things which, warmed over, are as acceptable as when first cooked. What more delicious than minced veal? (not hashed veal by any means); what more excellent than curried chicken? All curries may be made as well from cold meat. Of course, the general idea of hashed and stewed meat is justified by the wretchedness of it as usually served. Father Prout relates, that when young Thackeray was married and very poor, he asked some one piteously: "Can't you tell my wife how to hash mutton, that it may taste of something besides hot water and onions?"

As recipes for warming over meats are abundant, I will only say that the first necessity is to have gravy or soup to warm them in, and to heat the meat *very slowly*. The smallest family may have such gravy always on hand, by carefully saving cold gravy, or soup, and also by making stock of all bones, trimmings, and bits of cold meat, slowly stewing such fragments (bones must be cracked up) for some hours. When rich, strain and set by for use.

The only rules are:

*That the meat or poultry should stay in the gravy or stock* (or, if it must be, hot water with some sauce or ketchup for flavoring) *without boiling at all,* for some time, but steeping on the range, if not very tender already, it may so steep an hour or two. For this reason, *i. e.*, that it is never to boil, whatever gravy is to be made, if it is only from a fried onion, and flour and butter and water, it must be ready before the meat is added.

# CHAPTER X.

## A Few Rules for Making Bread and Pastry.

FOR the plainest family crust, as for the finest puff paste, the rule of light, cool handling holds good. For plain pastry, if you want it to be flaky, have your butter or lard very firm, your water ice cold, and *chop* the shortening into it. not too fine. If you do not want it flaky, but "short," *rub* the shortening in till it is like sand. Handle quickly and lightly. Just here perhaps some one will say, "I have a heavy hand, and can't handle it lightly." This is generally a mistake. By "light handling" is meant, to handle without pressure or squeezing. No woman would take new and delicate silk or tulle in her hand roughly; treat the paste as if it were some dainty fabric, and you will handle it lightly, and no matter how light the handling, let there be as little of it as possible, for the warmth of the hand will melt the shortening, which is one frequent cause of heaviness.

A cool hand is less at your command than a light one,—to dip the hands first in hot, then in cold water, will tend to cool them.

As regards shortening, I have said that for *flaky* paste
your lard or butter must be very firm; but the lard sold
nowadays is hardly firm unless the thermometer is at
zero—putting on ice does not make it so. Therefore if
butter is not to be used, it is far better to prepare your
shortening in the proportion of one-third lard and two-
thirds beef suet. *Beef* lard alone is better than this,
Fry out two pounds of suet, mix it with one pound of
lard, and when about half cold beat them together till
they are quite cold, working when you can no longer
beat, just as you would butter, pack it down and use as
lard for pastry. When you remember that beef fat is
the most nourishing and wholesome next to butter, and
lard the most unwholesome, you will see the advantage
of using it, independent of the facts that it makes
lighter paste and is cheaper.

Beef lard made from the *fat* of beef (not more than
one-third of which must be *suet* or it will be too hard,)
is as good as butter for every use but puff paste.

Puff paste is the most laborious work of the kitchen,
but when well done repays the effort. There are several
ways of making it, all producing the same result in the
hands of a skillful cook.

The French mode, which I prefer, is that in which
the butter is placed in a lump in the center of the paste
and rolled and folded until it lies in thin sheets or
"leaves" in the paste. The English (and usual ama-
teur) method, is to divide the butter and each time the
paste is rolled out to put on it a layer of small pieces.

Both result in excellent puff paste if well used; both
will fail if the process is not understood.

The quantity of butter being equal to that of flour,
the great object is to keep the butter from softening
while the paste is being made, for if it becomes softer
than the dough, it will not lay in the thin sheets which in
the oven produce the leaves characteristic of puff paste;
it will "break through" in rolling, stick to the board
and rolling pin, and as every break lets air out of the
paste, its lightness is reduced. To avoid this every
precaution must be taken. Let the flour be put in a
cold, dry place, (the reverse of what is wanted for bread
which must be dry and *warm*,) and have ice at hand unless it is winter, when, unless the kitchen is very hot, it
will not be necessary. The butter should be pressed in
a napkin to get out every drop of water, if very salt it
should be well worked under water in the napkin. The
dough should be wetted into a firm, smooth paste, and
*before* the butter is in it, it may be well worked and
beaten five minutes with the rolling pin, this helps to
toughen it so that the butter will less readily break
through. As I have said, the butter *must* be firm, but
it should not be harder than the paste, in very cold
weather, if it is so, work it till it is about the same
texture.

Any good directions for puff paste, of which there are
so many that I do not give them in a little book which
aims only to supply a missing link between you and
your favorite authority, will be very minute in its

instructions for folding and rolling, and if you wish to attain success you must follow these directions very closely; unimportant as I have known them to be considered, on their *exact* observance depends perfect pastry : every slovenly fold will tell on it. The leaves of puff pastry are really a matter for mathematical calculation. You are told to fold in three so many times and roll each time a certain thickness. You can see that three folds six times repeated would produce eighteen thicknesses with butter between each, but if you fold not in exact thirds but say one part laps only partly over, you diminish your leaves as well as let out the air. If in each of the six "turns," (as the professional term is, for such rolling out and folding,) you are equally inexact, even the most inexperienced will be able to see the difference it would make in the result.

There is a kind of pastry taught at the South Kensington school of cookery in London called "rough puff paste" so easy, so quickly made, and, with *exact* attention to details, so much better than average puff paste that it seems hardly worth while to undergo the fatigue of making the latter except for some special purpose.

For this valuable pastry I append the South Kensington recipe, with the warning, that if you do not pay scrupulous attention to the folding and rolling you may be disappointed and find you have excellent flaky light pastry, but no suggestion of *puff* paste. Properly made, however, there is very little home made puff pastry that will excel it, and it will rise from one to two inches.

But it is not enough to have pastry well made : it may
be bought from the best pastry cooks ready, but if you
do not understand *using it*, it will be spoilt.

When about to use it, roll it to half an inch thickness
for patties or pies, one third inch for tartlets.  If rolled
too thin it will not show its lightness, but will look mean
and poor.  *Never* press the paste, unless you are covering the *bottom* of patty pans, or of pie plates : there, as
you want to prevent the paste rising you may "deaden"
it by pressure, you may also press it to make it thinner at
this part leaving the edges thick and plump.  Trim the
edges with a clean quick cut of a *sharp* knife so that it
is not at all dragged, and do not touch the edge or border
with a finger.   If the pastry does not lie smoothly, never
mind, it will rise into shape.  To prevent the escape of
juice from pies, lay your finger round, just where the
fruit ends and the crust begins, forming a groove with
it, press firmly there, but *not at all* at the edge.   Above
all if you want a handsome pie and light crust don't turn
the edge over, as if you were *hemming* it.

South Kensington rough puff paste :

Take eight ounces of flour and six ounces of butter and put
them in a chopping bowl, chop the butter in the flour, not too
fine, make a hole in the center in which put the yolk of an egg.
Sprinkle over it a quarter of a salt spoonful of salt, and half a
teaspoonful of lemon juice, add a tablespoonful of ice water
and mix gradually and lightly with the ends of your fingers,
adding more water *if necessary* until it is formed into a *stiff*
paste.  Flour the board well, turn out the paste and any bits
of butter that have not mixed.  Flour hands and rolling pin,

roll out the paste till it is half an inch thick. Fold it in three, turn the rough edges toward you, roll again and fold in three, roll out, again repeat, making three times in all, it is then ready for use. This paste is excellent if made without an egg or lemon juice. If you can let it lie on the ice an hour it will be lighter.

## BREAD.

To make good bread you need fine dry *warm* flour, fresh yeast and the right consistency.

It is impossible to give an exact proportion of water and flour for bread, on account of the difference in quality of the latter, but as a general rule two pounds of flour to a scant pint and half of water will make a soft dough.

To each pound of flour allow one scant teaspoonful of salt, two full ones of sugar (if compressed yeast is used). Sugar may be omitted with slow working yeast.

The chief rules to remember are to have the dough just as soft as you can handle.

To dry and *warm* the flour, in all but really warm weather.

To dissolve the yeast in water only *blood* warm.

Water that seems far from scalding will yet be too hot for yeast.

Knead faithfully, using just as little flour as possible, it can be worked very soft without sticking, if you only just dust your hand for the first few minutes with flour.

Set to rise in a moderately warm place,—about 95 degrees, not hotter,—and keep from draught.

Do not attempt to make bread by any arbitrary rule

as to time, the only rule is to *let it rise till light*. If your book says two hours and it needs two and a half it will be spoilt if you obey that direction. Experience will enable you to judge by touch and sight when it is ready for the oven—but before that comes, you may notice the size of each loaf when you set it to rise, and don't put it into the oven till it is double that size even if it takes *double* the time your book directs. You may also tell by lifting a corner of the dough, if it looks swelled and is very tender to the touch, if it is full of fine little holes like a *very fine* sponge, it is light enough, if these holes are larger and coarse it is too light and you must knead it down well and let it rise again—but if you do not let it rise to more than double the original bulk it will not be too light, the holes will not be too large.

With these rules well in mind I think you will not fail in following any good recipe.

The rules for baking of all kinds are:

For white bread in small (two pound) loaves a hot oven in which you can bear your hand while you count 25 seconds. Time to bake one hour.

For larger loaves count thirty—to bake one hour and a half to two hours.

For all kinds of brown bread, count thirty.

For small puff pastry the oven must be hotter than for bread. You should be able to count twenty. Yet put the articles far from the fire that they may rise before scorching.

For Pies count twenty-five.

For Biscuit, rolls, and jelly cakes a very hot oven.

For cakes made with baking-powder and little butter a hot bread oven.

For cakes with more butter a little cooler oven.

For Pound cakes, a very moderate oven.

For Fish and all kinds of meat a hot oven. For small joints and birds a *very* hot one.

# CLEVELAND'S
# Superior Baking Powder

*Is made only of strictly pure Grape Cream of Tartar, Bicarbonate of Soda, and a small portion of flour, and does not contain Ammonia, Alum, Lime, or Acid Phosphates, and it is absolutely free from adulterations.*

*What other manufacturers impart to the public a knowledge of ALL the ingredients that enter into their baking powder?*

*Consumers have a right to know what they are using as food. In these times of extensive adulteration the public should demand this information, and in all cases where not given should refuse to purchase the baking powder.*

*CLEVELAND BROTHERS,*

*Albany, N. Y.*

# Good Housekeeping

## VOLUME FIVE,

## May 14th to November 12th, 1887, Inclusive.

In the detailed conduct of GOOD HOUSEKEEPING, it has never before had so rich a Bill of Fare to lay before its readers as the one prepared for Volume Five. A few of the most appetizing items of the different courses, may be named without prejudice to the many other attractive and well prepared side dishes, always awaiting a place on the Table of Contents.

## A NEW SERIAL BY CATHERINE OWEN.

Catherine Owen, with the initial number of Volume Five, commences a Serial of practical home life, entitled "MOLLY BISHOP'S FAMILY,—FROM BABYHOOD TO MEN AND WOMEN; A HOME STORY OF LIFE'S VISCISSITUDES." This Serial takes up the family of Molly Bishop, where it was left at the close of that very popular publication, "Ten Dollars Enough," and gives much interesting data and detail regarding the infancy, childhood, manhood and womanhood of the Bishop family, with practical lessons for the guidance of those who don't know, but would like to know, how the Children of the Household should enjoy health and long life and a wealth of riches, the value of which may not be estimated by the measurement or weight of gold and silver standards.

## HOUSEKEEPING IN FOREIGN LANDS.

1. "HOUSEKEEPING IN AN ENGLISH RECTORY," a very entertaining illustrated paper, is given in volume Five, written for GOOD HOUSEKEEPING by a resident of a charming English rectory.

2. "HOUSEKEEPING IN HONDURAS," with illustrations, prepared by an American, temporarily residing in Honduras, is another very attractive and appetizing diet on the Volume Five Bill of Fare.

3. "HOUSEKEEPING IN FLORENCE," with an illustration of the kitchen of the writer, who writes of her own observations and experiences.

4. "SWISS HOUSEKEEPING," by an experienced housekeeper and, at the same time, an entertaining writer.

## COFFEE MAKING AND COFFEE SPOILING.

"SIX CUPS OF COFFEE," prepared in response to an order from GOOD HOUSEKEEPING, for consumption in the Homes of the World, by the world's best authorities on the subject of Coffee Making,—

MARIA PARLOA,  CATHERINE OWEN,
MARION HARLAND,  JULIET CORSON,
MRS. HELEN CAMPBELL,  MRS. D. A. LINCOLN,

is the title of a group of papers more notable and of greater value to house-keepers than anything of the kind ever before published. These papers were all prepared for Volume Five.

## MEALS FOR THE MANY OF MODERATE MEANS.

A valuable and unique Series of papers under the above title for Volume Five, from the pen of Juliet Corson, one of the most experienced and authoritative writers on Cooking, who has had great success and won much fame by her practical writings, which are well represented by the title given to this Series of papers.

It is the purpose of the conductors of GOOD HOUSEKEEPING to make the Series valuable to all readers in the Homes of the World wherever found, par-ticularly so in homes where there are many mouths to fill and much anxiety of mind as to how to fill them comfortably, conveniently and healthfully, briefly expressed in the four simple words, " More Mouths than Money."

## TABLE SUPPLIES AND ECONOMIES.

The valuable department of "SEASONABLE TABLE SUPPLIES," so ably conducted by Mrs. Fannie A. Benson, for a season, several months ago, was permanently introduced in the first number of Volume Five with the addition of carefully prepared instructions for marketing economically and well,—giv-ing detailed information as to how to buy, what to buy, and when to buy, to the best advantage, having in view convenience, comfort, economy and health.

## PORTRAIT AND SKETCH OF CATHERINE OWEN.

Arrangements have been made for an early number of Volume Five to contain a portrait of Catherine Owen, who has had so many interested readers and won so many friends by her "Ten Dollars Enough," " Progressive Housekeeping," and other practical papers, to be accompanied by a personal sketch, prepared by the Editor of GOOD HOUSEKEEPING.

## QUIET HOURS WITH THE QUICK WITTED.

A new department for the Children of the Household, and the children of a larger growth, as well, under the title of "QUIET HOURS WITH THE QUICK WITTED," was added to the already well filled Bill of Fare of Volume Five. This consists of Acrostics, Anagrams, Games, Puzzles, Riddles, and the like, and to this department the "Quick Witted" readers of GOOD HOUSEKEEP-ING are invited to contribute. A "Query Box" is open at all hours of the day or night, for the reception of papers for this department, the only proviso in the premises being that everything submitted shall be fresh, bright and sparkling.

## THE PEDIGREE AND PURPOSE OF SOAP.

It has been facetiously said that "While there is life there is"—soap, to which might well be added, in all truth and soberness, this, that while and *where* there is soap, well and freely used, there is a life of cleanliness, not only next to Godliness, but keeping pace each with the other. From this domestic orthodox standpoint, two papers were prepared for GOOD HOUSEKEEPING on "THE USES AND ABUSES OF SOAP IN THE HOUSEHOLD," by Mrs. Hester M. Poole, who has given the subject critical and careful consideration, and whose valuable papers are always prepared and written with a view of doing "the greatest good to the greatest number" of those who are looking to and laboring for the interests of the Higher Life of the Household.

## ANAGRAMMATICAL ENTERTAINMENTS,

Our Anagrammatical Entertainments have been found so entertaining and popular, that GOOD HOUSEKEEPING's Anagrammatical Feast, and Anagrammatical Household Auction are followed in Volume Five, by an "ANAGRAMMATICAL GARDEN," in which issue Two Hundred and Fifty Cultivated and Wild Flowers, and House Plants were put up at Auction, with prizes for those who may be the first to name correct solutions that will be worth striving for.

The first number of Volume Five is enlivened by contributions in verse "appropriate to the occasion,—that charming writer of poesy and song, Clinton Scollard writing of "A Morn in Merry May," and Kate Putman Osgood of a "May Blossom," touching a reponsive chord in every loving mother's heart ; in addition to other poetic gems of springtime freshness and beauty.

In addition to this brief mention of choice selections of literary diet, the Bill of Fare for Volume Five is far richer and more appetizing than anything GOOD HOUSEKEEPING has spread before its readers, the parlor and sitting-room center tables, library desk, dining room and kitchen tables, pantry shelves and refrigerator, even, being loaded with articles of merit kept in waiting for a place in the pages of GOOD HOUSEKEEPING, and the Portfolio of Sundries has a never ending list of good things from which to draw, of MS. food from contributors, for the literary entertainment and sustenance of the readers of GOOD HOUSEKEEPING, in the Interest of the Higher Life of the Household in the Homes of the World.

GOOD HOUSEKEEPING gives it readers Two Volumes each year, of Thirteen Numbers each—Twenty-six Numbers a year. Subscription price $2.50 a year ; single copies Ten Cents, which may be had from the American News Company, or its agents throughout the country. Sample Copies, Ten Cents.

## CLARK W. BRYAN & CO.,

New York Office,                    Springfield, Mass.
290 Broadway.

**DYSPEPSIA.** Probably nothing adds so much to the misery of humanity as a disorganized stomach, and one who will give a return of good digestion is really a humanitarian well deserving of praise. Mr. JOHN H. McALVIN, who for 14 years was city treasurer and tax collector in LOWELL, MASS., has written a letter treating on this horrible malady that is well worth reading. It is entitled

"DYSPEPSIA, ITS NATURE, CAUSES, PREVENTION AND CURE."

Being the experience of an actual sufferer, and a conscientious study of the disease, it is especially valuable for dyspeptics, and those of sedentary or studious habits. He will send the treatise to any address free of charge.

# THE WORLD'S BEST.

## GARLAND OIL STOVE.

Odorless, non explosive. Has four 8-inch boiling places and extra large oven. Will do twice the work of an ordinary kerosene stove, and is therefore the **CHEAPEST** as well as the **BEST OIL STOVE** to buy.

### THE CELEBRATED
## BAY STATE RANGES.

First-class in every respect. Come and see them. Send for circular.

### BARSTOW STOVE CO.,
Providence, R. I.,
56 Union St., Boston,
230 Water St., New York.

## PERFECTION ATTAINED IN BAKING
### BY USING THE PATENT
## CENTENNIAL CAKE AND BAKING PAN.

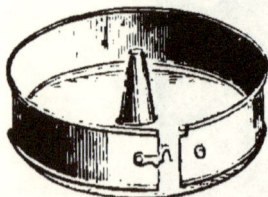

ENDORSED BY ALL PRACTICAL COOKS.

Side, Bottom, and Tube detachable. The Pan can be **unhooked** and taken from the cake. One 9 inch pan of **imported iron** and the Home Cook Book sent charges paid on receipt of **75 c.** Agents Wanted.

**THE CLIPPER MFG., CO., Limited,**          **CINCINNATI, O.**

# HYGIENIC

# COOKING!

The best preparation for

Housekeeping is a

# WIRE GAUZE DOOR,

As used exclusively on the

# NEW

# HUB

# RANGE.

# THE WIRE GAUZE OVEN DOOR.

is the most important improvement ever placed on a cooking apparatus. The gauze allows the outside air to be freely admitted to the oven ; the food thus being surrounded by a pure heated atmosphere during the process of cooking. More bread and of a better quality can be produced from the same weight of flour than by any other known process, while meats that are roasted in this oven lose scarcely anything in weight and retain all their juices. Meats cooked well done are as juicy as those cooked rare and *no basting* is required. Tough meat is made tender and palatable, while loaves of bread are larger than those cooked in a close oven, and keep fresh for a longer time. *Broiling* can be done more perfectly in the oven than over the live coals.

Astonishing as these statements may seem, their truth is vouched for by thousands of housekeepers in all parts of the country

Three of the New Hub Ranges, with Wire Gauze Doors, are used by the Boston Cooking School for their Demonstration Lessons, *being the only ranges used by them.*

Special circulars describing the remarkable effects of this door on the food cooked, together with a full explanation of the chemical changes and scientific facts involved, will be mailed on application.

SMITH & ANTHONY STOVE COMPANY,
52 and 54 Union Street, BOSTON, MASS.,
Manuf'rs of the Hub Stoves, Ranges and Heaters.

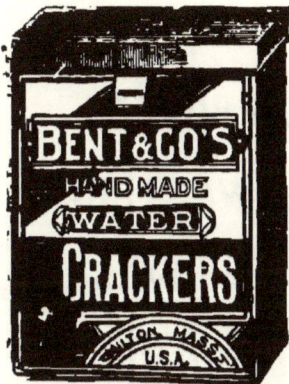

## THE CELEBRATED

# "ANDES" Range,

### PROVIDED WITH EITHER DOCK ASH OR DUPLEX GRATE.

The "ANDES" is a first-class range in every respect and is guaranteed equal to any other in every desirable particular or no sale. It can be had in the various styles, with high or low closet, cabinet base, with or without high shelf, with or without reservoir, and with dock ash grate. By a slight change it can be used to burn wood. Will keep fire continuously, bakes equally well at any time of the day. It is well made and tastefully finished in nickel and tile. Is handsome, durable and effective. Every Range fully warranted to do all that is claimed for it. Comparison of quality and price invited.

### MANUFACTURED BY

# PHILLIPS & CLARK STOVE CO.,
### GENEVA, N. Y.

Correspondence solicited.

www.ingramcontent.com/pod-product-compliance
Lightning Source LLC
Chambersburg PA
CBHW031746090426
42739CB00008B/901